TO SHE WHO WAITS

Bob Clyman

BROADWAY PLAY PUBLISHING INC
New York
www.broadwayplaypub.com
info@broadwayplaypub.com

TO SHE WHO WAITS
© Copyright 2019 Bob Clyman

Cover art by Doug Katz

First edition: November 2019
I S B N: 978-0-88145-858-9

Book design: Marie Donovan
Page make-up: Adobe InDesign
Typeface: Palatino

TO SHE WHO WAITS was first produced in New York by The American Renaissance Theater Comapny, running from 23 May–8 June 2019. The cast and creative contributors were:

HANNAH .... Lee Eden
JACK ....Brian Homer
MEG .... Carol Todd
SHEILA / MS PERRY / MOTHER BECCA......... Kathleen Swan

Director ....Maria Aladren
Scenic & costume design ....Joanna Conte
Stage manager.................................... Mackenzie McGuire
Assistant sound/music engineer.................. Abigail Nelwin
Assistant production manager........................ Alexis Wilner

CHARACTERS

MEG, 36; *bright determined woman, desperate to regain custody of her daughter; training to be a paralegal; a fairly recent émigré from a Christian community to the secular world*

HANNAH, 16; MEG's *daughter; still resides in the Christian community; a bright, angry girl who felt abandoned, when* MEG *left the community several years ago and angry now that* MEG *is seeking custody; has adopted her father's rigid religiosity, but her faith and emotional stability are under strain in response to her father's recent death and whatever temptation she feels from her mother's fight to win custody*

JACK, 38; MEG's *former husband and* HANNAH's *father, now deceased; flashback scenes reveal his progression from a good-natured, optimistic young adult who responded to personal failures and disappointments by finding new meaning in a extreme, "end days" religion*

The remaining three characters should be played by one actor: mid 30s to mid 40s

SHEILA, MEG's *attorney; bright, engaged, strategic; committed to fighting what she sees as "stealing other people's kids" by* HANNAH's *church*

MRS PICKETT, *a member of* HANNAH's *church community and officially* HANNAH's *church mother; while her thinking can be vague, odd or even psychotic, she has a strong moral compass*

MS PERRY, HANNAH'*s previous teacher; reasonable, caring; her close relationship with Hannah having been a casualty of* HANNAH'*s greater involvement with her church*

SETTING

Time: The present or near future. Flashback scenes range in time, beginning with MEg*'s adolescence, but all the others take place over the three years leading up to the present. Any scenes involving* MS PERRY *also occur during that period.*

Place: The play should move fluidly between present and past scenes in either McCullough County or Austin, Texas. The present action consists of either (1) a series of 12 court ordered visits between MEG *and her daughter* HANNAH *in a visit room at the McCullough County Courthouse or (2)* MEG*'s meetings with her attorney, Sheila, in an Austin law office. Scenes involving* MRS PICKETT *also take place in the visit room in the present.*

Staging / set requirements: Present scenes, with their more stable locations, should probably take place in specific, identifiable areas for the visit room and SHEILA*'s office, respectively, and both should be separate from the area where flashback scenes take place in order to minimize confusion over when a scene is occurring. There is one short present scene towards the end of the play that takes place in a courtroom.* HANNAH *will simply step downstage for this, and the text should be sufficient to identify the location.*

Ideally, scenes should flow seamlessly, with one of the characters in a scene simply turning to enter a different scene, either to express something to another character in that new scene or in response to an interruption by that character. Either way, the new scene will already be in *progress. All locations should be minimally suggested to support these rapid transitions. The actor playing three characters—*SHEILA, MS PERRY AND MRS PICKETT—*never appears in consecutive scenes, so she will have (admittedly little) time for a minor costume change.*

NOTE ON MUSIC

For performance of copyrighted songs, arrangements
or recordings referenced in this play, permission
of the copyright owner(s) must be obtained. Other
songs, arrangements or recordings may be substituted
provided permission from the copyright owner(s) of
such songs, arrangements or recordings is obtained
or songs, arrangements or recordings in the public
domain may be substituted.

ACT ONE

(A room in a court house annex for parent-child visits.
HANNAH *is wearing a modest brown frock. her hair is tied back and mostly covered by a bonnet)*

HANNAH: *(After a long silence)* When can I leave?

MEG: Twenty to three.

HANNAH: Twenty to three?!

MEG: Today is just forty minutes.

HANNAH: You mean I have to come back? *(Slight beat)* How many times?

MEG: Twelve. I thought your lawyer / (told you) …

HANNAH: What're we supposed to do for forty minutes?

MEG: Talk.

HANNAH: What for? You're just gonna lie.

MEG: When did I ever lie to you?

HANNAH: You should know, since you're the one who lied. Everyone knows you're a liar.

MEG: And by "everyone", you / mean…?

HANNAH: It doesn't matter who I mean, because it's everyone.

MEG: So which lie was the worst?

HANNAH: They were all equally the worst, because lying's a sin, and any sin's an affront to God.

(Responding to MEG's *slight, unintended sigh,* HANNAH *gives a mocking, exaggerated one.)*

MEG: Fine, I'll ask *you* questions. Let's see... Do you have a boyfriend?

*(*HANNAH *makes the sound of a loud buzzer.)*

MEG: What was that?

HANNAH: It goes off automatically when something's none of your business. Do *you* have a boyfriend?

*(*MEG *looks surprised.)*

HANNAH: Forget it.

MEG: I don't mind telling you. I just didn't expect / you...

HANNAH: Too late.

MEG: I don't know if you've pictured me drinking champagne on somebody's yacht / (but)...

HANNAH: I don't picture you anywhere. No one does. You're not a topic.

MEG: *(Slight beat)* For what it's worth, I've had one date since I moved to Austin.

HANNAH: They're still called "dates" at your age?

MEG: *(Viewing* HANNAH's *sarcasm as a hopeful sign)* Laugh now. Someday you'll be my age.

*(*MEG, *confused by* HANNAH's *smile, before realizing:)*

MEG: No, of course. Has God told Uncle exactly when he'll be here / yet?

*(*HANNAH *makes the buzzer sound again)*

MEG: We haven't talked in two years, Hannah. You must have *some* / questions.

HANNAH: *(Suddenly turns to an invisible microphone)*
Testing! *(Back to* MEG*)* My lawyer said they're
recording us so the judge'll know if you try to mentally
coercion me. How much time is left?

MEG: Basically all of it.

HANNAH: We have to stop at exactly forty minutes.

MEG: What are you doing then?

HANNAH: I just think we should follow the rules. If a
judge took the time to write "forty minutes"...

MEG: That's fine.

HANNAH: It might not make sense to *us*, but if
everyone just followed the rules they agree with...

MEG: Right.

HANNAH: I think rules are there to keep us from
veering off course and losing our way. Kind of...

MEG: I get it.

HANNAH: ...like a compass...get what?

MEG: You don't care what the judge thinks. You're
talking about the Bible.

HANNAH: *(Taking out her pocket bible)* I probably was...
being the Bible is the literal Word of God, and your
judge is just a fallen man who *thinks* he's God.

MEG: He's not *my* judge, Hannah. If anything / (he)...

HANNAH: Then why am I here?!

(Before MEG *can answer,* HANNAH *grabs her bible with
both hands and thrusts it in front of* MEG's *face. Beat)*

HANNAH: Liar.

*(*MEG *turns to* SHEILA *in her office.)*

SHEILA: She's tough.

MEG: At least I'm finally in a room with her. I've had three other lawyers, and none of them got me visits back. The moment my retainer was gone, so were they.

SHEILA: That restraining order was full of shit on so many levels, it took less than twenty minutes to get it thrown out. Visits were easy, but as far as getting you custody...

MEG: I wasn't expecting you / (to)... *(Indicating the office itself)* You're obviously way out of my price range. I barely came up with this / much... *(Taking an envelope stuffed with cash from her purse)*

SHEILA: Mike says you've been there eighteen months. What made you want to be a paralegal?

MEG: I didn't even know what a paralegal was. I just wanted something with more of a future than another waitressing job.

SHEILA: Mike and I go back to law school. He's a really smart guy, so when he told me there's a woman I should meet...

(Confused, MEG looks at SHEILA, expecting her to clarify)

SHEILA: Just to be devil's advocate, it's been three years since you left Hannah and two since you saw her...

MEG: I wouldn't say "*left*" / exactly.

SHEILA: Didn't you know you had only twelve months to show the court why you should get her back?

MEG: I never did anything to lose her.

SHEILA: The church says you abandoned her.

MEG: How's that even possible, when they wouldn't let me see her?

SHEILA: Did you explain that to the judge?

MEG: When? I had to move, and the letter saying the court date got mailed to my old address.

SHEILA: Then it was up to you to tell the court your *new* address.

MEG: I know that *now*.

SHEILA: There were only three things you had to do. Get a job, find a place to live and show up in court.

MEG: I didn't leave Jack till I had a waitressing job and a room with my sister in Brownwood.

SHEILA: Where you moved two more times in six months.

MEG: My first place got broken into, and my second... I'd never lived by myself...I didn't know how to look or what kind of questions / (to ask)...

SHEILA: Is this right? You're earning less now than you were as a waitress?

MEG: Yes, but once I get certified /...

SHEILA: What was wrong with being a waitress?

MEG: What was...? Nothing was *wrong*. My sister's a waitress, and she's the best person / I...

SHEILA: So was changing jobs and moving from place to place worth it, when you were supposed to be showing the judge you're stable?

MEG: It better be, or what was the point of leaving in the first place?

SHEILA: Good question. You grew up there, and *you* turned out okay, didn't you?

MEG: I turned out ignorant and scared. I was so afraid I'd fail at anything I tried, I'd've probably never left, except I wanted Hannah's life to be better than mine.

SHEILA: Yes. Excellent answer. I want to see more of that. *(Slight beat)* Oh, don't look at me that way. I didn't ask you anything her lawyer won't. You seem like a decent person, but I don't like you enough to give up the ridiculous money I usually get to represent you for free, unless you're the mother I need. So…are you?

MEG: You lost me.

SHEILA: *(Calling out)* Amy, give Meg another appointment as soon as I'm back from Chicago.
(To MEG, *as she pushes the envelope back to her)* In the meantime, put this towards rent. Now…tell me about Jack.

(MEG *turns to* JACK. *Flashback. 13 years ago. She's 16, he's 18.)*

MEG: Say it again.

JACK: I *really* like you.

MEG: You don't think I'm a slut for letting you?

JACK: After all the times we've done it, you're asking me now?

MEG: See, you *do* think I'm a slut.

JACK: I just said how much I like you.

MEG: *Now* you do. How long is *that* gonna last once your dad gives you his Malibu, and you can do it with any girl in McCullough County? Admit it, I'm just a passing amusement.

JACK: I've been liking you for *five years.* If you wanna know the exact day, I was turning sixteen…

MEG: *(Suddenly realizing)* Ewww!

JACK: What?

MEG: I was like *thirteen*… Perv! I didn't even have boobies then, I looked like a boy.

JACK: Grace Shroeder didn't start having boobies till last year, and now / she…

MEG: You haven't thought about *her* that way, have you?

JACK: No.

MEG: Liar. I've seen you stare at them. If that's how it's gonna be, tell me now. I don't want to wake up one day and find a note on how you and Grace Shroeder tried to resist / the…

JACK: Okay, I *have* thought about her that way, but you're the only girl I think about the other way too. The forever way.

(MEG *sighs, with genuine distress.*)

JACK: What's wrong?

MEG: Remember that time you didn't have a condom, and I was about to say "No, Jack, not without a condom", but then I forgot?

(*Long beat,* JACK *and* MEG *look at each other*)

MEG: Lucy Harris drove me to the same clinic *she* found out. (*Beat, trying to casual*) She thinks I should keep it. She said getting rid of hers was the worst mistake of her life. (*Beat*) What do *you* think?

JACK: She should've thought of that sooner.

MEG: I mean about *me*. Do you think I should keep it?

JACK: What kind of question…? (*He hugs her, then pulls back, afraid he did it too hard.*) You should be sitting down. Here.

(JACK *removes his overshirt and smooths it for* MEG *to sit.*)

MEG: How come you aren't mad?

JACK: The way I've been seeing our future, we'd've saved enough to get our own place and start having kids in two, three years anyway, so this just moves the plan up a little.

MEG: How long've you been seeing all that, 'cause this is the first I've heard.

JACK: How does it sound?

MEG: Off the top of my head, amazing. I kind of wish the timing…

(Beat, JACK waits.)

MEG: It was just an idea, but ever since Kroger gave me the extra shifts, I've been saving…

JACK: If you're worried about money, I was gonna surprise you later / but (I might as well)…

MEG: It was for college. I never told you, because after my dad wouldn't co-sign the loan…and it's not like the extra money…all I've saved in six months is enough for one course, so the whole idea was stupid…

JACK: Stop right there. What did we agree about you and negative thinking?

MEG: *(Slight beat, then conceding)* I guess I *was* doing it again.

JACK: So tell me this idea.

MEG: *(Beat, a twinge of excitement)* Well, Annie… works the register next to mine? …Someone at Central Community told her sister that after one semester, anyone with a B-plus average can get a free scholarship…

JACK: A B-plus for you should be easy as breathing.

MEG: …Except now, with the baby, there's no / way…

JACK: Whoa. Before you start in on some fresh line of negative thinking…I'll admit, the timing…I'm no expert on babies, but I've got enough nieces and nephews to know they take up most of the day…and since we'll eventually… Have you thought about how many you'd like, because I was thinking three.

MEG: This is amazing! That's the exact same number *I* want.

JACK: But *then* once they're a little older…

MEG: No, that sounds totally sensible.

JACK: Because you're the smartest person I know. *(Before* MEG *can protest)* You are. I'd still be taking algebra if it wasn't for you. And I'm glad you're telling me now, so we can add it to the plan.

MEG: So…what was my surprise?

JACK: *(Teasing)* It can wait.

MEG: You brought it up, so you *have* to tell me / now.

JACK: You win. Mr Lomax called me into his office, and after praising me for how many customers want me personally to service their trucks, he offered to bring me on fulltime.

MEG: Really?

JACK: *And* if I can broaden my skills to help grow the business, he'll consider staking me at some future point to my own garage. So I'm gonna need someone smart to manage the office and advise me on any exciting new business ventures. Could you see yourself doing that?

MEG: It sounds like a lot of responsibility, but if *you* think I can…

JACK: In fact, any planning type thoughts you have, this'd be the perfect time, while my brain is wide open.

MEG: No, it sounds like you've thought of everything.

JACK: I probably seem like the kind of person who nothing can stop me, but I wasn't always that way. When people said Mr Lomax has the best operation, but he's already got three drivers and two warehouse guys, the *old* me would've thrown up his hands and never even applied, but when I pictured your face if I got it…

*(*MEG *Suddenly hugs* JACK, *planting kisses all over his face.)*

JACK: Okay, enough celebrating…it's time to face the music. When does your dad get home?

(JACK, *sensing* MEG's *apprehension*)

JACK: Don't worry, *I'll* talk to him. You don't even have to be there.

MEG: What are you going to say?

JACK: How about… "Sir, I'm not gonna mince words. Your daughter's with child, but rest assured…I'm not the kind of man who walks away from a challenge."

MEG: *(Slight beat)* I guess that's good. It doesn't exactly make you sound happy.

JACK: Then how about "Sir, I love your daughter very much, and with your permission, I'd like to marry her?" Unless you think a wedding and saying you're pregnant are too much to throw at him in one conversation.

MEG: Did you just ask me to marry you?

JACK: I guess I did. You don't think he'll say no?

MEG: Not with me three months pregnant. Plus he's always saying what a fine, polite young man…Mr Lomax was telling him at church how "conscientious" you are, and my dad said the only puzzle is what you see in *me*. *(Beat)* It doesn't matter. Nothing before this second does. I'm with *you* now. How's this sound? *(Luxuriating over the words)* Meg…Thompson.

JACK: It does have a nice ring.

MEG: Meg Thompson.

(MEG *and* JACK *kiss, the hymn* How Beautiful *plays.* MEG *turns to* HANNAH *in the visit room. After another endless silence, a cough from the waiting room startles* MEG.)

MEG: Is that lady who brings you…Mrs *Pickett*… planning to sit out there the whole time?

HANNAH: She's not bothering anyone.

MEG: Doesn't she have chores?

HANNAH: She got up extra early to do them. I want her here.

MEG: Why?

HANNAH: In case you try to kidnap me.

MEG: Did she bring a gun?

(MEG *turns to face* SHEILA's *appalled expression.*)

SHEILA: Are you kidding me?

MEG: Oh come on… She knows I'd never…

SHEILA: Everything you say is being recorded.

MEG: She was just trying to make me look bad.

SHEILA: And now she has you on tape talking about a gun, so I guess it worked.

MEG: *(Slight beat)* I got angry, okay?

SHEILA: How often did Hannah see you get angry?

MEG: Jack and I fought, but we tried to control it around her.

(MEG *turns, as* HANNAH *speaks.*)

HANNAH: I wouldn't call it "fighting". It was more you yelling, and dad waiting for you to stop.

MEG: He didn't need to yell. He could just promise to pray for me, and that'd shut me up.

HANNAH: Do you remember dragging me out of the Fisher Price store by my hair?

MEG: *(Directing this as much to the microphone) Once,* Hannah. And I must've apologized a hundred times in the car.

HANNAH: Dad would never have done / that.

MEG: Dad is dead!

HANNAH: Don't say that!

(MEG *turns to* SHEILA, *who is shaking her head*)

MEG: You're right, there were better ways, but *someone* had to say it. If she wants to believe Jack was a better parent, she's entitled, but she needs to understand I'm her *only* parent now, and she belongs with me.

SHEILA: If the judge asks you your first reaction when you heard Jack was dead, what'll you say?

MEG: To be totally honest...

SHEILA: Wrong answer. You say Jack was a good man, and you tried to make it work, but the differences were too great. Do you think you can say that?

MEG: Yes.

SHEILA: Good.

MEG: It's true.

SHEILA: Even better.

MEG: The funny thing is Jack didn't start off any more religious than me. When Uncle came and started preaching about the dark final days ahead, I just thought we should try a different church, but Uncle's preaching spoke to a need in Jack I never knew he had.

(MEG *turns to* JACK. *Flashback*)

MEG: That was Mr Lomax.

JACK: Tell him I'm sick.

MEG: Just talk to him, Jack.

JACK: I can't.

MEG: You've got nothing to apologize for. He's the one that went back on a promise.

JACK: He never promised. He said if I showed him I could grow the business, he'd stake me, and I haven't. Everyone raves how I keep their trucks running, but if I start to explain how much they'll save by turning their old fleet over for lighter trucks, their eyes go… and then yesterday…God, what an idiot…I said if he's having second thoughts about staking me to the full amount, I could get by with half, and he said "Jack you're gonna need the other half, and who else is gonna risk that kind of money on you?"

MEG: *(Slight beat)* Jack…you're the best box truck mechanic around, and Lomax knows that. You need to take more pride in what you do well.

JACK: It's not just work. Nothing's gone the way we planned. Hannah's great, but we should have *three* by now.

MEG: That was just a happy number we picked, because we liked the sound.

JACK: What if we're being punished for something we did?

MEG: You heard Dr Bennett, it's my uterus.

JACK: What does *he* know?

MEG: Probably a lot from all those years he went to medical school.

JACK: Too many things've gone wrong to just be a coincidence.

MEG: The problem with our plan, Jack…it wasn't really a plan. It was just us wanting the same things everyone does, and not everyone gets them.

JACK: Do you ever think God might have a different plan for us?

MEG: I guess I think…if he does have a plan for us, it's the kind most people get.

JACK: Because we're nothing special?

MEG: Not to him, but you're special to me. We chose each other out of everyone. *(Beat)* I love you, Jack.

JACK: I love you too, Meg. But that can't be all there is.

(MEG turns to SHEILA.)

MEG: Then...ten days after our pastor died, Uncle arrived. Jack was on his lunch break, when a tall, weathered man appeared, striding right down Main Street...preaching to everyone he passed about he-goats and beasts from the sea, and when he waved for them to follow, Jack thought...why not?

JACK: *(Picking up the story, excited, now as a flashback)* He'd been planting corn when God told him to throw away the seed...leave his entire life behind...and go warn everyone the end times were near. So he began to wander...stopping in every town. Crowds would pack into large tents to listen...rich people offered to build him a church...but he always went back to wandering, until one night he fell into a fever dream, where he was lost in an unfamiliar town, when suddenly a kind stranger pointed to a church. Everyone there was standing by an open grave, weeping, and he began weeping too. He'd never seen a church that plain and unassuming, or felt what he was feeling...that he was finally home. Then he woke up and wandered ten more days, until this morning when he saw the same unassuming church...*our* church, Bountiful Blessings. Then I realized his dream was the same night pastor died.

(JACK, amused that MEG and HANNAH aren't quite buying it:)

JACK: I know *(what you're thinking)* ...and that was *my* first reaction, but the more I listened... *(Slight beat)* This town has always been the closest thing to nowhere. Remember when you said we're not even part of God's plan?

MEG: Just not a special part.

JACK: Well, I was starting to agree, but a man like Uncle doesn't settle in a place like this by accident. He was sent for a reason.

(MEG *turns back to* SHEILA)

SHEILA: How *did* you react when Jack came home with that story?

MEG: Where I grew up, stories like that were normal. Things like Jesus rising out of his grave...no one had a problem with that, and this wasn't much of a leap. It's easy to say I should've seen this coming, the way Jack was starting to change, but he was still *Jack*, and *everyone* thought the world was ending, it was only a question of when.

(MEG *turns, as* JACK *speaks. Flashback*)

JACK: You have to admit Uncle's sermons are livelier than Pastor Campbell's. It took a hundred extra folding chairs this morning to sit everyone.

MEG: I miss the choir. No matter how dull Pastor Campbell got, I always loved the music.

JACK: That was the problem. It was *so* beautiful, some people came just for that. We all loved the choir. Uncle grew up listening to hymns on the radio to fall asleep, so he loved it as much as anyone, but if it didn't bring us closer to God...

MEG: It did for me.

JACK: I know adjusting to him hasn't been easy. He can be abrupt and short-tempered, but he didn't come here to kick back with people. His job is to help us get ready, and like he says, if some people want that kind of pastor, Verity Baptist is just a mile down the road.

MEG: The Harrises took him up on that.

JACK: If they had just asked themselves what he might be trying to teach us...like I'm suggesting with you and the choir...

MEG: I did that, and I still don't know what I'm supposed to learn from being deprived of music.

JACK: How to wait. How to hear God in the silence. Remember how the music always came in right after the sermon...like we needed a reward for sitting through it...and then one Sunday it was gone? No pretty music telling us when to leave or what to feel. People hated that, but now, like this morning...nobody wanted to leave. Everyone sat there in silence like they were all one person...waiting for him.

MEG: I tried to sit like that, but I got distracted by how everyone near me had a slightly different way of breathing. While I was wondering why that's so, I began to notice my own breathing, which was *kind* of interesting, but then I wondered if I was being vain by showing *too* much interest, so I just sat there and waited till it was time to go.

JACK: Well...sure, that fits. You've always been curious. For some people, questions and being into logic are the only paths to God.

MEG: And that's okay? I'd love to know there's a good reason praying is harder for me.

JACK: Try *this* on for logic. If you're in a room full of friends you've known your whole life, and they're all feeling *one* thing, but you feel something else, which is more "logical" ...they're just imagining God is in the room, or you're shutting him out?

MEG: I *want* to let him in. I see what it's done for you. How confident... You're so different with Hannah. When she told us that endless story about Anita Becker's problem losing weight, you listened all the

way through and made some very helpful suggestions.
I wish *I* could be that patient.

JACK: God can help with that. As long as you keep
one door open…you'll never know why he chose that
moment any more than why no two people breathe
alike…but he'll come.

(JACK *kneels down, beckoning* MEG *to join him. She
hesitates, tempted, then turns as* SHEILA *speaks.)*

SHEILA: "Just one door open." Hannah kept hers open,
and God came in. What can *you* offer her compared to
that?

MEG: I'm her mom.

(MEG *turns, as* HANNAH *speaks:)*

HANNAH: I don't need another mom. I already have
Becca and Tammy.

MEG: Who?

HANNAH: Becca and Tammy…my church moms.

(Confused, MEG *turns back to* SHEILA.)

SHEILA: For the past year, Uncle's been contacting
families where the parents can't cope…they're on the
verge of losing their kids…and encouraging them to
sign the kids over to the church, so they can be raised
in a good Christian home instead of being dumped
in the system. Then he picks two women as church
mothers for each one and performs a "scriptural
adoption", so when God comes, the kid won't be left
behind.

MEG: Those adoptions aren't legal, are they?

SHEILA: They're not *illegal,* and he's done over thirty.
Eventually it won't sound as weird or scary, so we
need to show people *now* that scriptural adoption is
just another name for stealing someone else's kid.

You're the first parent who's been willing to fight them. Unfortunately, Hannah's willing to fight too.

MEG: But if she's still a minor...

SHEILA: Most judges feel a sixteen year-old should get to choose.

MEG: Even if the choice is between her mother and a cult?

SHEILA: *You* see a cult. This judge sees an angry adolescent, whose devoted, single father was awarded sole legal custody by the Texas Family Court. So if she wasn't kidnapped, and no one's forcing her to stay....

MEG: Does brainwashing count?

SHEILA: If you mean Hannah's bought into some alternate universe of lunatic ideas, because it's all she's ever exposed to, that's called "growing up in a family".

MEG: But they're *not* a family. They can call themselves "Mother Becca" and "Mother Tammy" all they like. Hannah's got *one* mother, and that's me.

(MEG *turns, as* HANNAH *speaks.*)

HANNAH: I also have twenty-seven church brothers and sisters.

MEG: *(In a lame attempt to sound positive)* Wow.

HANNAH: You're just jealous, because you have an abnormal yewverus and could only have one.

MEG: Must be hard in the morning when everyone has to pee... *(As she turns quickly and defensively back to* SHEILA:*)* What was I *supposed* to say?! *(She turns back to* HANNAH*)* So which one's your favorite?

HANNAH: I love all of them *equally*. That's how *real* families are.

(MEG *turns back to* SHEILA.*)

SHEILA: Any brothers or sisters of your own nearby? Judges like that.

MEG: My sister, Tina's, the only one who still talks to me, and she's two hours away.

(As MEG shakes her head no to each:)

SHEILA: Aunts…uncles…? Cousins?

MEG: Look, I'm sorry I don't have a big loving family that dotes on Hannah. My *friends* are my family. I just spent Christmas at Mike and Caren's. It took two extra leaves to fit us all around the table.

SHEILA: You mean "Mike from work" Mike? So it was mostly people from the office.

MEG: Don't say it like that.

SHEILA: Like what?

MEG: Like it doesn't *count*. Would the judge feel better if I picked someone up at a bar and spent Christmas with *him*? At least she'll *have* a Christmas with me.

(MEG turns to JACK. Flashback)

MEG: You can't take them back. I bought those presents for *her*.

JACK: Meg, it's one thing to celebrate out of ignorance, but now that we know it's wrong…

MEG: What's the point of being Christian, if we can't even celebrate Christmas?

JACK: Christmas was invented by *pagans*. It's just an excuse to spend money.

MEG: I know…that's the *point*. She can't even celebrate her birthday. Hannah deserves one day a year when everything stops, but it *doesn't* end, and *she's* the center of the universe, not God.

(MEG turns as SHEILA speaks.)

SHEILA: What about "special" friends? Has there been anyone else since Jack?

MEG: Between school and work, there's no time.

SHEILA: Someone at work, then. How about Mike? He's put on a few pounds since law school, but he's still a good looking man.

MEG: Are you serious?

SHEILA: Not your taste?

MEG: He's exactly my taste. He's also Caren's taste, and she *married* him.

SHEILA: You ever think *he* might be interested?

MEG: As in why else would he hire me?

SHEILA: You're offended.

MEG: Yes.

SHEILA: Unfortunately with you, "offended" comes off as petulant, which isn't attractive. Do me a favor and stop falling into every trap I set for you.

(Beat. Clearly stung, MEG takes out several photos.)

MEG: I just put a deposit on a nice two bedroom. This one's her room. She'll be able to watch the sun set from her window. Maybe if you ask her lawyer, she won't just tear them up.

(MEG hands them to SHEILA. Slight beat)

MEG: I'm sorry I keep disappointing you.

(MEG turns, as JACK speaks. Flashback)

JACK: I'm not angry, Meg, just disappointed.

MEG: I'm trying, Jack. If it was just a few of our friends… Why can't I be saved without the whole church watching me?

JACK: I was afraid, "What if I get up there, and God sees a gravy stain on my shirt and decides not to take me" …but the moment I felt the water, every fear about not measuring up washed away, because in spite of all my failings, I was perfect to him.

MEG: I mean, *that* part sounds nice, Jack, but what if I get up there, and nothing happens?

JACK: If you really want it to / (happen)…

MEG: You know I do. I want to surrender all my fears like you…and what makes it even harder… You're an important person here, Jack. I see how Uncle depends on you, and everyone else looks up to you, so when your own wife can't even…I know they talk.

JACK: They're concerned. They know anyone can have a sudden case of nerves, but when they see you struggle every Sunday…

MEG: I just wish they'd leave you out of it.

JACK: These are our friends, Meg. Maybe if you didn't keep things bottled up…Ed was telling me Ruth got so nervous when *she* was saved, she spent the whole week before throwing up. I know she'd be happy to talk with you.

MEG: Tell Ed thanks, but… In fact, don't say anything, I'll speak to Ruth myself. It's not your job to fix me, and if they think / (it is) …

JACK: I don't care what they think, Meg. I'm worried what *God* thinks when every time he offers salvation, you turn him down.

MEG: He knows I'm doing the best I can. He's seen me usher…pull weeds near the chapel…

JACK: And everyone appreciates…but we're not the kind of church you can just show up for an hour and stack a few chairs.

MEG: What's wrong with that kind of church? *This* church used to be that kind of church.

JACK: Don't forget, you have a daughter.

MEG: (Confused) Right. Well, what do you mean?

JACK: How're you gonna feel if your eleven year-old gets saved before you? Her friend, Bethany's, getting saved on her birthday, and Hannah's three months older.

MEG: They're completely different kids.

JACK: What was she saying when I got home?

HANNAH: (Interjecting, as MEG continues talking with JACK) Don't swallow your tongue.

(MEG, laughing, then responding to JACK's baffled expression)

MEG: She meant that girl who got saved at Verity Baptist.

HANNAH: Just as her head rolled back, she started making those Holy Spirit noises like Gramma, but the new pastor didn't see her mouth was open and kept shoving her head in the water.

MEG: I thought she told you.

JACK: Do you think if I knew this was at Verity Baptist… Did you even try to stop her?

MEG: The girl invited her… They're friends.

JACK: Never mind, I'll speak to her.

MEG: Come on, Jack… Let her be a child. What does being saved even mean at her age? Most of the girls just do it to please their parents. Once she's older, but for now I want her to feel she has options.

JACK: Like what?

MEG: I don't know. What if she wants a different kind of life?

JACK: Like what?

MEG: I don't *know*. There was a time…if you heard a story about a girl who nearly drowned from speaking in tongues while she was getting baptized, you'd've fallen down laughing.

JACK: Before I got saved, I'd've been *telling* that story. I'm a different man and a better father.

MEG: I agree. But between your job and church council meetings, you're busy. Hannah's my only job. She's what I do all day. So please…don't tell me how to do my job.

(MEG *turns, as* HANNAH *speaks.*)

HANNAH: I have no idea what you did all day. I just know you never did anything with me.

MEG: (*Trying to mask how stunned and hurt she is*) I see. So I didn't…for example…read to you every night before bed?

HANNAH: When I was *four*.

MEG: You don't remember us reading every Harry Potter book, starting when you were *nine*?

HANNAH: At most it was one or two, since you were always out.

MEG: "Always out"? Where?

HANNAH: All I know is you got home really late.

MEG: And dad put up with that? (*Slight beat*) Remember that blue Oldsmobile he had? The A C gave out once right before we went to Hugo, and the drive was like a two hour steam bath? Why didn't we take my car instead?

(HANNAH *looks away.*)

MEG: Exactly. We had one car. Dad let me use it for errands, but that was it…so how did I get to wherever I was gallivanting all night? (*Indicating the microphone*) Is all of this just so the judge can hear? You can't possibly be this confused.

HANNAH: That's how I remember / it.

MEG: I was *there*, Hannah. Every parent-teacher night…every camp-fire outing and Easter bake sale… Did I ever miss a volleyball match?

HANNAH: Dad went to my matches, too.

MEG: I know, he and I went together.

HANNAH: Then stop acting like you're so great, and everything bad was his fault. You're the one who left.

MEG: You're right, and we can talk about that, but I never stopped loving you. There hasn't been single day (that)…

HANNAH: No, *dad* loved me. He stayed. *(Slight beat)* Remember that saying you got from grandpa? Something to do with the post office.

MEG: Whenever he left work for the day, he'd tell his customer, "Rain or shine, I'll be back"…

HANNAH: Just like the post office. You said it right before you left, but you never came back for me. You think you can leave me like a piece of furniture you couldn't fit in the car, then show up three years later, and I'll still be in the driveway, waiting for you? *(She takes out a small plastic baggie, filled with torn pieces of MEG's apartment photos and dumps them)* Why did you even *have* me? I'll bet if this was Oregon…I read about a woman there who had two liquor drinks and wound up conceiving with a man she met that night. When she got her abortion, a pretty nurse took her to a bright, cheerful room with gentle music from her favorite hymns, and every two minutes the nurse would squeeze her hand and say the baby was better off. Now this woman's richer than a pharoah from flying around the country and telling other women abortions can be fun.

MEG: *No one* thinks abortions are fun. If whoever wrote that really believes / it...

HANNAH: Every sentence is a proven fact.

MEG: I've never heard *any* woman say she had church music piped in for her abortion.

HANNAH: She's not gonna tell *you*. If people found out what's really going on / in...

MEG: You know what? It's fine. We don't need to waste any more time discussing it.

HANNAH: You think murdering infants before they're born isn't worth discussing?

MEG: There are so many things we *need* to discuss, and so far / (we haven't been able) ...

HANNAH: Any time someone gets close to what the abortion lobby is / up to...

MEG: Christ!

HANNAH: Apologize for saying / that.

MEG: Can't you hear how *ridiculous* you sound?!

HANNAH: Finally. Go ahead and say it. You hate me.

MEG: No, Hannah. As hard as you're trying to *make* me hate / you...

HANNAH: I could always tell when you were hating dad. Your face got boiling hot like now.

MEG: What do you mean? My face isn't...

HANNAH: Feel it!

MEG: I don't know what / (you want me) ...

HANNAH: Feel your face!

(Suddenly HANNAH *brings her own face inches from*
MEG's. *She then raises an open hand as if to strike, causing*
MEG *to flinch, before pressing it hard against* MEG's *cheek.)*

HANNAH: Feel! *(Just as suddenly, she pulls away, throws
her head back and shouts at the microphone.)* We're done!

*(*MEG *turns to* SHEILA.*)*

MEG: She doesn't understand. I never planned on
leaving without her. But when I called a lawyer, he
told me no judge in south Texas would allow a wife
to run off with her husband's child because of some
differences over religion, and if I tried, I'd probably
end up in jail. So I forgot about leaving and tried to
make the best of things at home.

*(*MEG *turns to* JACK, *who has been waiting for her.)*

JACK: Brace yourself. Jed Gray's will was read today,
and apparently he left his farm...all ninety acres...
to the church. Uncle wants to start building houses
by March. By his count, even if we lose a few more
families to Verity Baptist, at least a hundred will come,
and if each gets a third of an acre, we'll still have over
twenty left to farm on. When Uncle told me, I said "It
certainly couldn't have come at a better time for me
and Meg".

MEG: I don't know what you're talking about, but we
have a house.

JACK: A very nice one, and we've been fortunate to
spend / (so many years there) ...

MEG: How many houses around here have a front
porch this big and are walking distance to Hannah's
school...?

JACK: I can't think of any, but you're missing the point.
We both know something has to change...when Uncle
told me his plan, I nearly flew home to tell you...but

then Pete pulled up with the mail, and I saw this letter for you. *(He takes out a crumpled letter from his pocket)*

MEG: You opened my mail?

JACK: You weren't home, and it looked official.

(JACK, holding up the letter for MEG to see. A couple of beats)

MEG: I didn't want to tell you till I found out my grades.

JACK: A "B-plus" and an "A". Today is too important for us to ruin it fighting, but I did wonder. All those evenings I'd get home, and you'd be on the computer, is *this*...?

MEG: Was there even once your dinner *wasn't* on the table, or a pile of dirty clothes / was...?

HANNAH: *(From off-stage)* Could you two please...?!

MEG: It's okay, honey...dad and I are just disagreeing.

JACK: How did you pay for them?

MEG: Birthday money.

JACK: From who?

MEG: Different people...your mom for one.

JACK: I thought she always gives you a sweater.

MEG: She does, so last year I asked for money instead. When gave me another sweater anyway, I took it back, along with every tin of smoked meats and assorted jellies...

(JACK gives a small, grudging laugh of recognition)

MEG: You agreed. When I told you I was pregnant, you said if it wasn't for the timing...

JACK: *You* brought up the timing...

MEG: Right, and I *wanted* to stay home with her, but I assumed once she didn't need me every second, I'd be able / to...

JACK: To do what? Put her in day care, so she could get molested? You remember what happened to / that girl...

MEG: Someone we knew could've watched her. My mom...your mom...

JACK: Except they're not *her* mom...you are.

MEG: *(Beat)* I may as well say this now. Central Texas Community is less than forty minutes, and if they accept me, I intend to go.

JACK: How? We've got one car, and I need it for work.

MEG: Then I guess we'll have to sit down like other married people and figure something out.

JACK: Like what?

MEG: Like get a second car.

JACK: As in take out a loan? No thank you.

MEG: Most jobs pay more if you have an Associates Degree, so I could pay it off quicker.

JACK: I didn't realize there's a demand for people who took "Native American Poetry".

MEG: I just wanted to take one course purely out of interest, before I buckle down.

JACK: And you're interested in that?

MEG: It just... You know what's sad? I don't even know enough to know what interests me.

JACK: *(Slight beat, softening)* You were always curious. And smart. I'm surprised you only got a B-plus in that other...

MEG: "Intro to accounting."

JACK: *(Slight beat) My* subject was history.

MEG: I remember.

JACK: I always liked reading about people who invented things no one thought they could.

MEG: Maybe there's a class on that. I could check.

(JACK gives a short laugh)

MEG: Why not? I can totally picture you with a first day haircut and brand new pencil. Come on, it'd be fun. The three of us sitting at the table with our books open.

JACK: I'd be the one with his book upside down.

(JACK and MEG laugh. The gift of a warm, if fleeting, moment)

MEG: I need this, Jack.

JACK: *(Beat, softly, with a sense of regret)* You've always had your own way of thinking...it's one of the first things I fell in love with...and for all the times people told me I could show my love better by *correcting* some of those thoughts, I've mostly resisted, because they're so much a part of you.

(MEG turns to SHEILA.)

MEG: I thought that went pretty well, considering. So well, I could almost imagine...I mean, Jack had never stopped loving me, and maybe now that he understood how important...

(JACK calls to MEG. Flashback)

JACK: Meg...

MEG: *(Still to SHEILA)* ...so when Central Texas accepted me for the fall / (I thought) ...

JACK: We need to finish that conversation.

(MEG turns back to JACK.)

JACK: There are things I never told you...things I couldn't until Uncle was absolutely sure. *(Slight beat)* God made him a promise. If he could gather a hundred families, who'd be willing to leave their homes to wait with him, and forty innocent children, so they wouldn't be left behind...then he would come for us...and as a sign he was near, he would consecrate a special place that he would call the Realm for us to wait.

MEG: I'm not moving, Jack. If you want to wait for God, I'll wait with you, but we're doing it from here.

JACK: When God is this clear about his plan and what he expects from us in return, then any plans of our own devising, like college, have to be set aside.

(Beat. An impasse. Then, as if suddenly aware of her surroundings, MEG's eyes fix on something.)

MEG: Jack... Where is the computer?

(MEG turns back to SHEILA.)

MEG: When I called a different lawyer and said I *have* to leave, he said Jack must realize he can't raise Hannah alone, so if I could reassure him he'd still see plenty of Hannah by letting him keep her while I moved...but once I got there, the judge didn't like it that Hannah had to share a bedroom, and the cheap health insurance I had through work wouldn't let me add her, and the three weeks she was supposed to stay turned into months, but I still saw her every week. Then Jack started making excuses...

SHEILA: Did you ever tell Hannah that *Jack* canceled the visits?

MEG: No.

SHEILA: How about why you left him in the first place?

MEG: I didn't want to turn her against him. She still had to live there.

SHEILA: If she didn't know basic facts like those... At least tell her now.

MEG: Why? So she can accuse me of waiting till he's dead and can't defend himself?

SHEILA: *(Trying to control her frustraton)* Do you know why I chose *you* to help me stop this church? You clearly love your daughter, and no matter how many times the system screwed you over, you never gave up, but mostly it's because there was no one else. So tell me right now... Should I wait for a different mother, or are you the mother I need? *(Slight beat)* You have eight more visits. Then either Hannah picks you, or Mothers Becca and Tammy get to keep her. Nothing you've tried so far is working, so next time, get it right.

(MEG *takes this in, then turns as* HANNAH *speaks.*)

HANNAH: I brought these, so you'll see how even physically we're nothing alike.

(HANNAH, *thrusting a photo in front of* MEG:)

HANNAH: Compare this one...to these. I always took after dad.

MEG: You think?

HANNAH: Yes, I *think*. So does everyone.

MEG: When's it from?

HANNAH: That trip we rode horses.

MEG: Right...we took a ton of pictures there. It looks like you're having fun in this one.

HANNAH: I had more fun in the pictures with dad.

MEG: There was a great one of you whupping me at horseshoes. And another of us competing over who could finish her blue raspberry snow cone first without getting a brain freeze.

HANNAH: I don't remember.

MEG: Well, I'm glad you kept *one* picture of us.

HANNAH: I didn't *keep* it. I just never bothered to throw it out.

MEG: *(Looking at a different picture)* You definitely have his eyes. Is that what people mean by you look like him?

HANNAH: They mean I look the same way *every* way like him.

MEG: Hold your hand up in front of you.

HANNAH: Why?

MEG: Just the left one, and take a really good look at your fingers.

(HANNAH hesitates, then shrugs and does so.)

MEG: Now look at mine. *(Raising her own right hand to mirror HANNAH's)* I'm just bringing it closer so you'll see how much our fingers are alike.

HANNAH: They're *nothing* alike. Yours are weird looking. *(Pointing to MEG's)* See how they go along, and then all of a sudden they stop.

MEG: They "stop"?

HANNAH: I can't believe no one's ever told you.

MEG: That my fingers suddenly stop?

HANNAH: Maybe not "stop" exactly, but they're way shorter than mine.

MEG: They just look shorter, because they're farther from your eyes. If I bring them closer…

(MEG, *moving her hand slowly towards* HANNAH's *until they almost touch. For a moment,* HANNAH *watches as if mesmerized, before jerking her hand away.)*

MEG: Now clasp your hands, so your thumb's on top, and I'll do the same, but first we both have to turn away, so we can't see what the other's doing. *(She turns so her back is to* HANNAH.*)*

HANNAH: This is stupid.

MEG: Are you ready?

(Sighing perceptibly, HANNAH *complies.)*

MEG: I'll give you any odds your right thumb's on top of your left.

(Stealing a glance at her hands, HANNAH *quickly drops them to her sides.* MEG *turns, her right thumb on top.)*

MEG: I'm not psychic. Some people always keep their right one on top, while others like dad…

HANNAH: So what? There's only two ways a thumb can go.

MEG: I don't know if your new school believes in "genes", but there's a gene for that. Remember how hopeless we were when dad tried teaching us to curl our tongues like a cloverleaf? He liked to joke that his family caught flies that way. There's a gene for that too. There's even a gene for hating cabbage.

HANNAH: I don't want my hands to look like yours.

MEG: There's a lot you can change, Hannah, but you can't have a different mom. *(With sudden enthusiasm)* I'm hungry. What do you feel like for lunch?

HANNAH: Mrs Pickett brought food.

MEG: You mean that teeny plastic bag with a few string beans and a sorry looking plum? I noticed the sandwich shop you used to like, Proud Eagle, delivers now.

HANNAH: I don't eat things we didn't grow.

MEG: Uncle always said if you need to be in the world, it's okay to partake of its pleasures, so when you return, you can honor God by renouncing them again. You still like tuna on pumpernickel bread?

HANNAH: "Pumpernickel"?

MEG: That's what you always asked for. And no mayonnaise. Remember telling off that waitress at Friendly's for slathering it on, after you reminded her twice?

HANNAH: You mean most people don't mind when a total stranger puts whatever she feels like on their bread?

MEG: No, I admired that. I'm just making sure I have your sandwich likes and dislikes straight. *(Beat)* It doesn't have to be a sandwich. There are a hundred and twenty-two items on the menu to choose from, and I'd be happy to go through each of them, if you want / me (to) …

HANNAH: Just get me a tuna sandwich with nothing on it.

MEG: *(Phoning before* HANNAH *can reconsider)* Hi. I'd like to order a tuna sandwich for delivery to the courthouse?

HANNAH: And tell them whole wheat. I don't know where you got "pumpernickel" from.

MEG: To drink?

HANNAH: Just water.

MEG: Stop it.

HANNAH: *(Slight beat)* They probably don't have root beer.

MEG: Do you have...? They don't.

HANNAH: Then get me a coke. With lots of ice.

MEG: *(Into phone)* Yes, lots of ice.

HANNAH: Tell them regular, not diet.

MEG: You get all that?

HANNAH: And some French fries.

MEG: You still make those curly fries with a little paprika? *(Listening, then giving a thumbs up to* HANNAH*)* And I'll have the same as her. That's Hannah Thompson...in the annex.

*(*MEG *hangs up. Beat.* HANNAH *is looking away.)*

MEG: You remember what I used to make tuna with?

HANNAH: No. *(Beat. Then yielding)* Fresh dill. *(Beat)* Before you left, dad took you to a really nice place for dinner, and he looked...happy...but when he got home... What did you say to him?

(Sound of rain. MEG *joins* JACK *in a restaurant. Flashback)*

MEG: I'm glad you thought of this.

JACK: I figured once you leave on Friday, who knows when we'll / have (another chance) ...?

MEG: It's actually Thursday now. My new boss said one of the girls is sick, would I mind, and since he's gonna try give me Wednesdays for my regular / day off...

JACK: Listen, if something comes up, and you need to come a different day...

MEG: I think whatever day we choose, we should try and stick to it. I don't want to confuse her any more than she already… Sorry. I know you're trying to make things easier / for me.

JACK: No, you're right. This is why you're a great mother. You always think of these things.

MEG: *(Slight beat)* So the plan is I'll pick her up from school, take her somewhere for a few hours and get her home in time for bed.

JACK: Any idea where you'll take her? *(Quickly reassuring)* I just mean that's a lot of time, and if it's pouring like now…

MEG: We'll figure something out.

JACK: If it's easier, you can see her at the house.

MEG: Won't you be there? I mean it's nice of you to offer, / but…

JACK: You know, it wouldn't be the worst thing if she saw us actually getting along.

MEG: You don't think that could give her the wrong idea?

JACK: Like what?

MEG: Like it isn't over. *(Beat)* Just so we're clear, I'm really glad you suggested coming here, but it doesn't / mean…

JACK: I know. *(Beat)* We should've come here more often. You used to say "Come on, it's been awhile since we laughed", and I'd say "We can't, it's too much money". I should've listened more. That's one of the things I've learned since I started going to Two Equals One.

MEG: This is what I was afraid / of.

JACK: I wish you'd come with me. We don't just read from the Bible.

MEG: Jack...I know you want me to stay, and now that it's our last night...so I understand why you're trying so hard, but...and I need you to hear this...it's having the exact opposite effect on me.

JACK: Why do have to use words like "last chance" and "over"?

MEG: You're the one who wanted everything clear and in writing.

JACK: That was the church's lawyer. I didn't even *want* an agreement. If that's why you're upset, say the word, and I'll tear it up.

MEG: Jack, please...

JACK: Do you need me to beg?

MEG: You've been so great these last few weeks. It's the closest I've felt to you / in (so long) ...

JACK: Then put off the move. Just for a week.

MEG: I already promised. Why would you ask me when you know I can't? Are you trying to make me hurt you?

JACK: I didn't plan to ask, but when you walked in, you looked so beautiful...I keep thinking you can't hurt me any worse than you already have, and every time I'm wrong. *(Turning to unseen waitress)* I won't be staying.

MEG: You don't have to go. We can still have dinner. Don't go.

JACK: You eat...I'm not hungry. *(He stands, takes out his wallet and leaves some cash.)*

MEG: I think you're right. It *would* be nice for Hannah to see us getting along. Why don't I come in for a few minutes on Wednesday when I drop her off?

JACK: My lawyer thought somewhere public like the parking lot near Kroger's, so there's no chance of trouble… Drop her there.

(MEG *turns and goes to* HANNAH. *It is their first flashback scene. They are standing away from the house, next to her borrowed car, as* MEG *puts a last box in the car.*)

HANNAH: Mom? if I liked some boy, and he asked me out, and then we got married…

MEG: This boy doesn't happen to be Daniel?

HANNAH: Who?

MEG: On your bus, with the dimple…the two of you pass notes back and forth?

HANNAH: We don't pass notes. He passes notes to *me*, and I barely read them.

MEG: Sorry. So the two of you get married…?

HANNAH: But then we have a huge fight and break up. If you liked him, and *I* broke us up, would you be mad at me? Because Gramma was talking to dad, and she sounded mad at *you*.

MEG: *(Considering how to answer)* When two people break up, the one who leaves always looks like the villain, and nobody likes a villain.

HANNAH: She's your mother. She's supposed to keep liking you no matter what.

MEG: Gramma didn't stop liking me. She *never* liked me.

HANNAH: If you can't stay with her, isn't there anyone closer than Aunt Tina?

MEG: Brownwood's only an hour.

HANNAH: Aunt Helen's fifteen minutes.

MEG: Between Uncle Joe and the boys, her place is already tighter than a tin of sardines. *(She turns to*

SHEILA.*)* I tried Aunt Helen, but she reacted just like my mom, and as for friends... Even if one of them *wanted* to put me up, none of their husbands would've let me in the house.

SHEILA: Did you tell Hannah you asked, and everyone said no?

MEG: Helen was her favorite aunt, and my friends... their kids were *Hannah's* friends. She saw those people every day, and they treated her like their own. I didn't want her lose that, just because they stopped liking me.

SHEILA: So she didn't know why you left or why you moved so far. For all *she* knew, you decided to bust up the family, like that lawyer said, over some squabble about religion.

HANNAH: *(Interrupting, still next to the car in flashback)* If dad's so terrible, how come you're leaving me with him?

SHEILA: See?

MEG: *(Turning back to* HANNAH*)* Whatever problems dad and I had, you're his shining star, and he loves you like nothing else. You may need to remind him to check your homework and remind yourself when it's time for bed, but you're old enough now...I probably did too much reminding, so it might even be... And one thing I'm sure of...you'll always get plenty of hugs and tickles, and he'll never do anything on purpose to hurt you. *(Turning back to* SHEILA*)* How do you tell a thirteen year-old as you drive away that her father *and* her church are crushing your soul, and you need to get her out, before they crush hers too?

*(*HANNAH *is holding up a yellow dress she took from a box)*

HANNAH: I like it. You always look pretty in yellow.

MEG: It's gonna be my interview dress. Do I look professional?

HANNAH: Very. Find something soon, okay?

MEG: You won't have to wait long, Hannah. I promise.

(JACK *steps onto porch, pointing at his watch, before going inside.* HANNAH *and* MEG *laugh like conspirators.*)

MEG: You should go in.

(*Neither moves. Then* MEG *hugs her fiercely.*)

MEG: Rain or shine, Hannah, I'll be back for you.

(MEG *turns, as* SHEILA *interrupts, more gently now*)

SHEILA: She was probably wondering "Why won't you take me *now?*"

(HANNAH *has returned to the visit room.* MEG *joins her.*)

MEG: Do you remember right before I left, when I asked you to wait? If I could go back, I'd say, "Let's just leave... We'll figure the rest out tomorrow."

HANNAH: I did wait. Even when I was praying, I always kept one ear out for you. Everyone told me you'd given up. Then you moved to Austin, and they said it proved you weren't coming back, but I *still* waited. Until one I day I started to pray, and my attention wasn't divided. I could finally give all of it to God, and I knew I'd stopped waiting. It didn't matter anymore if you came, because someone who never broke a promise and loved me more than I could even imagine was coming instead.

MEG: I had no right asking you to wait. You were so young, a day must've felt like a year...but the thing about God's love, Hannah? Mine is *real*...and no matter what anyone told you, I never gave up. I promised I'd be back, and I'm here. Now it's up to you. If you tell the judge you want to live with me / then...

HANNAH: I can't! (*Beat*) You waited too long. I can't.

(Beat. They continue to look at each other. SHEILA *steps towards* MEG, *then smiles.)*

SHEILA: **Better!**

END OF ACT ONE

ACT TWO

(Sound of phone. Lights up on MEG *and* JACK. *Flashback)*

MEG: No, I can call her "any time". Read the agreement.

JACK: Any time "within reason". Not six, when we're about to eat.

MEG: Fine, I'll call back at seven.

JACK: Seven is homework, and we're busy after that. Try back tomorrow.

HANNAH: *(Shouting from offstage)* Tomorrow's Wednesday!

JACK: *(Still to* MEG*)* I forgot… We'll be out.

MEG: You're always out. And what's she doing out on a school night anyway?

JACK: I signed her up for group.

MEG: What group? You don't mean that (group) … "The Straighter Path"?

JACK: You're the one who wanted her to talk about it with kids in the same boat.

MEG: Yes, that nice Banana Splits group at school, which you pulled her out of the second I left. Not in some basement getting lectured every night on how God hates divorce.

(Interrupted by HANNAH *from the visit room)*

HANNAH: I learned a lot there. Remember that yellow dress you bought before you left? One night someone asked me what it cost, and I realized I was the only kid in group whose mother came out on top.

MEG: Wait. You think I did better than dad?

HANNAH: *You* didn't have to give money to a mortgage person each month…

MEG: I guess dad never explained how a mortgage… When you buy a house, …you pay the bank a small… you remember percentages?

HANNAH: What's that got to do with making dad pay the whole amount?

MEG: He paid the whole amount, because he kept the whole house. I could've made him sell it and pay me half, but I wanted to keep things the same for you as much as I could. If I had known the bank would end up selling it for a fraction / of *(the cost)*…

HANNAH: That wasn't his fault. He was in pain all the time.

MEG: I know. And if he would've just admitted the reason…

(MEG *turns, as* JACK *interrupts her. Flashback)*

JACK: Stop using that word. It's not a disability.

MEG: You need to start taking this seriously, Jack. You had a stroke.

JACK: Even the doctor said it was mild.

MEG: For a *stroke.* He also told you to schedule a complete workup to find out why you had it.

JACK: Who said you could call my doctor anyway?

MEG: I didn't. Hannah called *me* and read the entire medical report. Why'd you show it to her?

JACK: All I said was "Maybe it'll make more sense to you than it does to me".

MEG: Apparently it made just enough to scare her half to death, that's why she called. Tell Dr Bennett you need a thorough workup and bring that report with you.

JACK: I see Dr Wood now.

MEG: From the church? Call Dr *Bennett*. And then call Human Resources. You only have thirty days to send back the disability forms. Ask for Connie, and if she isn't in... Are you writing this down?

JACK: Let me put Hannah on, you can tell her.

MEG: I'm telling *you*.

JACK: You know how I am with forms. Hannah's smart that way like you.

MEG: It's not her job...and you need to start learning these things. You have a great disability plan, so get them the forms.

JACK: I'm not looking for a handout.

MEG: You'd rather have Hannah come home after school every day to take care of you?

JACK: I told her I'm fine, but she won't listen.

MEG: Because she sees you're *not*. You can't leave that decision...she's a kid.

JACK: She says she'll just worry more if she isn't / home.

MEG: I don't *care* what she says, it's not her job.

JACK: I know, it's yours!

MEG: *(Beat)* It doesn't have to be hers *or* mine. That's why you *have* insurance. I need to / go.

JACK: Wait. *(Beat)* Is it okay to ask how you are?

MEG: Do you remember what you said when I started to tell you / last time?

JACK: I didn't mean that. I don't want you to fail. I mean, I do, but...

MEG: I know. You were just hoping I'll change my mind.

JACK: Is that such a terrible thing to hope? *(Beat)* Admit it...you miss me a little.

MEG: I can't afford to go there, Jack. I need every drop of energy to keep looking ahead.

JACK: *(Teasing)* That sounds like a yes.

MEG: *(A small laugh)* You always were a hard man to discourage.

JACK: I know you weren't happy, Meg. Are you happier now?

MEG: I guess I'm doing about as well (as I could've) ... *(Beat, her struggle more with herself now)* It's just a lot harder than I thought.

(MEG *turns, interruped by* HANNAH, *on phone. Flashback)*

HANNAH: Austin?

MEG: I never planned on moving there. I assumed Brownwood, with all the new office jobs, but with no experience...so when I heard Austin was having a job fair, where companies from all over Texas...I got more interviews in two days than six months in Brownwood, because some places care more about the kind of person you are. They asked me what I hope to be doing in five years instead of just have I ever been to prison?

HANNAH: How far is Austin from here?

MEG: Two and a half hours. *(Before* HANNAH *can speak:)* I know, but I'll still come every Wednesday...and you could spend some weekends here.

(JACK *enters.*)

JACK: What's your mom talking about?

HANNAH: She met some man at a fair.

MEG: Tell dad you're supposed to have privacy when I call.

HANNAH: Mom said I'm supposed to have privacy.

JACK: Tell her I just came in to get something,

HANNAH: Dad said he just came in / to…

MEG: I heard.

HANNAH: Whose car'll you use, now that you won't have Aunt Tina's?

JACK: What happened to Tina's car?

HANNAH: Nothing. Mom's moving to Austin.

JACK: Austin?! Does she have any idea what she'll be spending on gas?

HANNAH: Dad asked if you have any idea…?

MEG: Tell dad I'll talk to him when we're finished / (but right now) …

HANNAH: Mom said she'll talk to you when we're…

(JACK *gestures he's leaving and quickly goes*)

HANNAH: He left.

MEG: So how does staying with me for weekends sound? You're old enough to take the bus.

HANNAH: What if dad needs me? You know he isn't well.

MEG: I wish the timing…but there's never gonna be a good time, and you'll still see plenty of dad. This is what we talked about, Hannah. A better life. Austin has so many opportunities. What are you going to do back there when you're a grownup?

HANNAH: Dad said God'll take us way before that, so
I don't need to worry. If you could see how exciting…
Twelve more families broke ground last week, and
new ones keep showing up. There's a man who spent
his entire life in Ohio writing books, but after he heard
Uncle speak, he tore up every page he ever wrote and
moved to the Realm. Someone else dreamed he was
sitting down to supper with his son, who drowned last
year, when a huge bird with bright, knowing eyes flew
in and perched on the sideboard…so the man jumped
in his car and drove all night to ask Uncle if this was a
sign.

MEG: Hannah…

HANNAH: Dad's putting a huge front porch on our new
place, because he knows how much you loved the one
here, so when we move to the Realm next month…
You've never even *seen* it mom. I think if you came
back and tried again…

(JACK *returns*)

JACK: Let me talk to your mom now.

(JACK *Takes the phone, gesturing for* HANNAH *to leave. She
starts to go but then dawdles, staying within earshot*)

MEG: I'm sorry for springing this on you, but it
happened so fast…

JACK: Why now? We've been getting along better. The
last two phone calls…

MEG: I agree, but if I want to give Hannah a decent
life, those jobs are in Austin, and this way, I can start
helping you more. I'm sure having Hannah 24/7, isn't
(easy)…

JACK: I manage.

MEG: Of course you do…but why should you have to? Maybe once we decide on high school, we can meet somewhere and figure out a schedule…

JACK: What do you mean "high school"?

MEG: The school district where I'll be just won a blue ribbon for being excellent. It'd be a waste not to send her, and this way you could have her for fun times like the summer.

JACK: Summer's our busiest season. I have to fight Lomax for a single day off.

MEG: I'll do my best to be flexible, but you're gonna need to start being more flexible too.

JACK: I *have* been flexible.

MEG: Not really, Jack. You promised if I ever had to miss a visit because of work, I could see Hannah a different day.

JACK: I can't tell her to cancel plans she already made.

MEG: Like changing a sleepover that wasn't for another two weeks? People move, Jack. You're moving to the Realm in a month, and I haven't said one word / about…

JACK: Right, except I'm moving fifteen minutes, not three hours, and there's no way I'm making her sit on a bus for three hours, just so you can live in Austin.

MEG: I haven't fought you, Jack…whether it's canceling phone calls…taking her to Bible class four nights a week…or even getting her baptized after you agreed in writing…

JACK: Sorry for trying to keep a Christian home.

MEG: Bullshit.

JACK: Excuse me?! I'm sure people use words like that all the time in Austin, which is another reason she's not going.

MEG: Why don't we wait and see what the *judge* thinks?

(Beat, MEG sensing JACK's anxiety:)

MEG: You're not giving me any choice.

(JACK hesitates, then takes out a small recording device, bringing it close to the phone.)

JACK: If you think a sleepover's a flimsy reason for canceling, wait till the next time you ask.

(As JACK starts to record the call, HANNAH, who has been listening, moves towards him, looking pointedly at him.)

MEG: I'm through being reasonable.

JACK: Is that a threat?

MEG: If you try to stop me from seeing her, it's on you.

JACK: It *is* a threat.

MEG: Just make sure she's there when I come on Wednesday .

JACK: Or you'll do what, grab her off the playground?

MEG: If it takes that. I will do whatever I have to…

(JACK quickly hangs up and stops recording, as MEG continues speaking.)

MEG: You know instead of fighting, we should be discussing how to make this…Jack?

(As JACK looks away, aware that HANNAH is staring at him, MEG looks at her phone, realizing that he has hung up.)

JACK: *(Finally looking at HANNAH, defensive)* What? *(Beat, softening)* The lawyer said people who make threats almost always deny them later, and unless there's proof…

(Beat, HANNAH *looks away.)*

JACK: I don't feel good about doing this either, but what choice…? One minute your mom's saying "Austin", and the next she's ready to sign you up for school there. It's not right. *(Beat)* You know, I've been assuming you want me stop her, but maybe I'm wrong. So before I take this any further, just tell me… Would you rather live with mom?

(JACK *goes to* MS PERRY. *Flashback)*

PERRY: Mr Thompson… It's a pleasure to finally meet you. Thank you for coming in.

JACK: My daughter's education is very important to me, Ms Perry, so anything I can do to help.

PERRY: Please call me Gail.

JACK: My parents taught me to respect teachers, so with your permission, I'd prefer Ms Perry.

PERRY: I don't know if you're aware, but there's something new on our website, so you can see what Hannah has for homework and roughly how long it should take her.

JACK: We don't have a computer. Don't you tell kids the homework while they're here?

PERRY: Yes, but what if Hannah is sick that day?

JACK: Hannah doesn't get sick. She dresses warmly, I see to that.

PERRY: *(Slight beat)* How long does she usually spend on homework? Yesterday, for instance?

JACK: She finished it on the bus.

PERRY: *(Showing* JACK *on an printout)* Here's what she was assigned. Altogether, it should've taken her ninety minutes. If she's only on the bus for twenty…?

JACK: That's Hannah. I'm always telling her not to rush.

PERRY: And you're sure she did it. Did you actually see her put it in her knapsack?

JACK: My daughter's not a liar.

PERRY: No, but she *is* a teenager. Hannah's smart enough to get by without even trying for now, but if she wants to take honors classes in high school...I'm sure you and Mrs Thompson agree that / it's...

JACK: I had to put a restraining order on Mrs Thompson, so as far as I'm concerned, she doesn't belong in this conversation.

(PERRY *is clearly surprised*)

JACK: Why are you giving two hours of homework to fourteen year-olds anyway? She's got Bible class four nights a week, and that takes...

(JACK, *reacting to* PERRY's *expression:*)

JACK: Do you have a problem with Bible class?

PERRY: I just didn't realize how many nights. It might explain how tired she looks in the morning.

JACK: I was advised when a girl's mother abandons her, a strong moral education is the only way to keep her from going down the same road.

PERRY: I understand. I'm just thinking, if she went *two* nights a week, she'd still be / (getting) ...

JACK: This advice came from people who could give you a dozen reasons why if there's anywhere she should be spending less time, it's public school.

PERRY: Well...maybe we can agree to disagree on that one.

(*As* PERRY *turns to walk* JACK *out:*)

JACK: I don't know if you're aware, but Hannah's been saved.

PERRY: She still has to do her homework.

(As JACK leaves, MEG goes to PERRY. Flashback)

MEG: I don't understand. The school's been great about sending me Hannah's report cards, but I keep calling to see why I didn't get the last one, and no one's returned (my calls)...

(Having looked to see if anyone else is in the hall, PERRY gestures quickly for MEG to enter.)

PERRY: Jack came to see me, and it didn't go well. The next day, he was back with a lawyer.

MEG: He told the judge I threatened to kidnap Hannah. I haven't seen her in five weeks.

PERRY: I'm guessing you haven't heard what she scored on the Statewides.

(PERRY turns to HANNAH. Flashback)

PERRY: All I told her was by scoring in the top ten percent, you won a two thousand award to help pay for college later, and she wanted to know why your dad turned it down.

HANNAH: It's none of her business.

PERRY: Then maybe you could tell me, because I think it's a mistake.

(HANNAH sighs at having to explain the obvious)

HANNAH: Any time the government gives you a handout, it's gonna have strings attached.

PERRY: Like what? (Slight beat) No, I'm genuinely curious, what kind of strings?

HANNAH: They never say till you sign something, and then it's too late.

PERRY: Hold on, I'm getting the dictionary, so we can look up "handout".

(PERRY *finds it, then beckons* HANNAH *to sit next to her*)

PERRY: Could you read this to me?

HANNAH: "A portion of food, clothing or money, as if given to a beggar."

PERRY: Now here.

HANNAH: "Implies the recipient is undeserving."

PERRY: "The recipient is undeserving." Unlike an *award*, which you won.

(PERRY *leaves.* HANNAH *stays, re-reading the definition, then turns to* JACK.)

JACK: Guess what? New Beginnings Day School called, and there's an opening...you start tomorrow.

(HANNAH *turns to* MEG, *who is now in the visit room*)

MEG: Ms Perry was the only person I could call and find out if a friend hurt your feelings...or which president you chose for your book report...or just something funny you said. When dad pulled you out and sent you to New Beginnings...

HANNAH: That's still no excuse for what you did.

(MEG *turns to* SHEILA.)

SHEILA: You did understand that the judge *specifically* added "New Beginnings" to the restraining order when Hannah started there, so you couldn't go anywhere it?

MEG: The order said "No closer than three hundred feet", / and I never...

SHEILA: "Three hundred"'s just a number. It means "Don't go near her, *period*".

(MEG *turns back to* HANNAH.)

HANNAH: Do you have any idea how embarrassing...? Everyone *saw* you!

(MEG, *shifting attention rapidly between* SHEILA *and* HANNAH, *trying to fend off each one's reproaches:*)

MEG: I didn't realize from where I was standing / (that)...

HANNAH: Someone yelled, "Look, it's Hannah's mother". Then *everyone* was at the window...

MEG: I needed to see you. I thought if I'm three hundred feet and only stay ten minutes...

HANNAH: My teacher kept saying, "Why is your mom here? She's not supposed to be here". I told her "I have no idea who that lady is...she's not my mom".

SHEILA: Any chance you had of getting visits back after a stunt like / that...

MEG: I needed to see her!

SHEILA: All they had before was a cut off phone call recorded by an angry ex. *You* gave them a stalker mom on a silver platter.

MEG: I made a *mistake*! I made lots of them, you've been more than clear on that, but I still thought... Hannah *knows* me. Once everyone calms down, she'll realize...

(MEG *turns to* HANNAH, *in what is now a flashback.* MEG *seems confused but hopeful, almost bouyant*)

MEG: I don't understand. Obviously, I'm not complaining, but I assumed if you wanted a visit the judge would need to write a new order *(allowing)* ... How did you get here? Does dad...? No, of course, he'd have to know...and he's okay with this?

HANNAH: It's not a visit.

(HANNAH *hands* MEG *a sealed envelope.*)

HANNAH: This is from the doctrinal council. They're desanctifying you. Read.

(MEG *hesitates, then opens then envelope and reads.*)

HANNAH: Do you understand what it means? Your name'll be erased from the Book of Judgment.

MEG: *(Finally looking up)* Do you understand what it'll mean for *us*?

HANNAH: There won't be an *us* anymore. *(Beat, then suddenly)* You've had a whole year to seek correction... What did you *expect*?! *(Slight beat)* It isn't final for three more weeks. A lot of people are praying you'll show contrition, so they can kneel beside you again. If you'rel not ready to make a full confession, the council can work out a penance plan.

MEG: *(Beginning to understand)* Did dad ask you to come here and offer me a deal?

(HANNAH *seems genuinely stung to hear it put that way*)

MEG: You're fourteen years old, and he's using you... Can't you see how wrong that is?

(*As* HANNAH *gets up to leave,* MEG *backs down.*)

MEG: What sort of penance plan?

HANNAH: *(Taking out a page of notes)* When you go before the council, they'll explain, but the main things... First, you have to apologize for going to my school and promise it won't happen again.

MEG: I'm sorry, and I promise.

HANNAH: No, in writing. Next. You have to get right with God and accept his bountiful blessings.

MEG: Get baptized, you mean. *(A couple of beats)* All right. Tell dad I'll find a pastor who does full body immersion, but it can't be Uncle.

HANNAH: I'll ask, but I doubt Uncle will think it's enough.

MEG: I'm not asking to be raptured up to the same cloud as him. Just an hour a week with you.

HANNAH: Finally…you have to acknowledge you sinned against God by abandoning me.

MEG: I didn't abandon you.

HANNAH: You don't have to repent…just admit you did it.

MEG: If I did, I don't deserve visits.

HANNAH: You can call it some other word in your head, but in the agreement…

MEG: No. I won't agree and certainly not in writing.

HANNAH: Even if this is the last time you'll see me? *(Slight beat)* Do whatever you want. I don't / care.

(MEG, *shouting after* HANNAH, *as she leaves:*)

MEG: Wait! Tell dad that Uncle can baptize me himself. But I *never* abandoned you.

(HANNAH *continues to the visit room, where* MEG *follows her, still speaking, in the present.*)

MEG: I'm sorry, but dad was wrong. He should never've put you in that position.

HANNAH: Who said it was dad? He didn't even *want* me to go. If you could've seen him after you met with the council…

MEG: Go on. If I'm being unfair, tell me how.

(HANNAH *hesitates, then turns to* JACK. *Flashback*)

HANNAH: So she lied?

JACK: She admitted to everything she couldn't deny, but anything like saying how much she loves you, where no one could prove it's a lie, Uncle could tell she was making them up.

HANNAH: How could he tell?

JACK: The same way he can read signs. He just can. *(Beat, as he casts a sidelong glance at her)* To be honest, they didn't sound like lies to me, but everyone else on the council...and when nine different people agree...

HANNAH: It must be hard to disagree, when Uncle's opinions are straight from God.

JACK: It can be. When he brought up erasing mom from the book six months ago, I *did* say I thought we should give her more time, but what I really *wanted* to say was as hard as certain things are to forgive, denying someone the right to God's grace is so final, maybe we should leave that decision to *him*, because once *we* start making it... We all know churches that did, and before long, all it took was a single careless remark...

HANNAH: *(Beat. Reacting to his unfamiliar intensity)* Are you okay?

JACK: I finally said it. I said "Before we vote today, there's something I need to say", and I said it. Then Uncle said this was the second time I'd asked the council to go easy on her, and I should be mindful of what could amount to a pattern.

HANNAH: *(Beat)* What did the council say?

JACK: There was nothing *to* say.

HANNAH: I wonder if that's why Mr Becker...?

(JACK looks HANNAH, a little surprised.)

HANNAH: When he picked Anita up earlier, he seemed...different. *(Beat)* How come she changed? Mom wasn't always bad like she is now.

JACK: You shouldn't call her that. For all we know, she could change back and walk through that door tomorrow... *Then* how would you feel?

HANNAH: Do you really think was telling the truth about how much she loves me?

JACK: It sounded that way to me.

HANNAH: Then why did she leave? It's nice here. God wouldn't've picked it for us to wait, if it wasn't nice. All her friends were here. *We're* here. *(Beat, as she struggles with a question)* I know I'm nothing like mom...and I really try to be good...

JACK: *(Beat)* What is it, Han?

HANNAH: Do you think it's possible when I'm a grownup, I could start acting like her?

(HANNAH turns back to MEG in visit room.)

MEG: Do *you* think it's possible?

HANNAH: No. Let's just play. *(Taking out a stack of cards)* Unless you're afraid, which you should be, because I'm going to beat you by a landslide.

MEG: Go ahead, pick a card. I might be a little rusty / (but) ...

HANNAH: You didn't forget to bring them?

MEG: Would I do something like that?

(MEG takes out a bag of M & Ms and pours some into a bowl. HANNAH picks a card and reads.)

HANNAH: "The soothing tongue is a tree of life..."

MEG: "But a perverse tongue crushes the spirit." *(Imitating the sound of a bell and gesturing in triumph)* Just like riding a bike. *(She takes an M & M and eats it with exaggerated relish.)* Ask me another.

(HANNAH picks another card.)

HANNAH: "The discerning heart seeks knowledge…"

MEG: *(Mumbling this several times to herself, then confident)* "But the mouth of a fool feeds on folly." Now you. *(Grabbing another M & M, she starts to pick a card.)*

HANNAH: The cards make it too easy. The way I like to play is you need to remember the whole proverb and say *both* parts right. Like… "All the days of the oppressed are wretched, but the cheerful heart has a continual feast". And you get two M & Ms for that. *(Grabbing two M & Ms and popping them into her mouth)* Now you.

MEG: *(After some effort, excitedly thinking of one)* "Idle hands are the devil's playthings, and idle lips are his mouthpiece."

(As MEG reaches for reward, HANNAH makes buzzer sound.)

HANNAH: That's Proverbs 16. We're only doing 15.

MEG: Okay… Let me think.

HANNAH: *(After a couple of beats)* Mom.

MEG: I'm *thinking. (Beat)* So not "idle hands…"

HANNAH: There are twenty-three to choose from.

(As MEG struggles, HANNAH is already gloating)

HANNAH: Give up?

(HANNAH reaches to take the entire bowl as her prize)

MEG: Wait, I know where… This has everything. If you want look up a proverb in Swahili…

(MEG takes out an I-pad. HANNAH looks away.)

MEG: It won't bite you.

HANNAH: A couple of boys had them in public school. We're not supposed to look.

MEG: You're not supposed to eat French Fries either, but last time you scarfed down all of yours and then ate most of mine. The rules are different here, so try to think of something that would be fun to see but not a sin if you saw it. *(Beat, an idea)* I know. Remember when you used to ask me this?

(MEG types a question and hits enter. HANNAH stares.)

MEG: These blue things are called links. Click on any one of them.

(MEG, realizing HANNAH is lost:)

MEG: Okay, it's time you learned to scroll.

(Taking HANNAH's finger, MEG begins to guide it.)

HANNAH: *(After slowly scrolling for about ten seconds)* How can there be so many answers to one question?

(HANNAH clicks on a link. As she stares at the screen with wonder, a loud knock startles her, as if it were a judgment on her interest. MEG touches her reassuringly.)

MEG: That must be our food.

(MEG leaves, then quickly returns with it. HANNAH starts setting two places to eat. The division of labor is so automatic, there's a sense they always did it this way)

HANNAH: Would you say grace with me this time?

MEG: Sorry. The church kind of spoiled that for me. Go ahead, I'll wait.

(HANNAH closes her eyes in a brief, silent prayer. HANNAH and MEG eat without speaking for several beats.)

MEG: There are times…like after a really good day at work, I'll go home…turn on some music…make myself a nice little dinner…and suddenly I'll have an overpowering urge to thank…*someone*. But the things I'm grateful for never seem because of him.

(HANNAH *and* MEG *eat in silence.* HANNAH *thoughtfully sips her Coke, then begins to crack an ice cube in her mouth.*)

MEG: What *is* it with you and ice?

HANNAH: We don't have any. We just pick whatever we'll eat that day, so it doesn't have to keep.

MEG: You want mine?

HANNAH: (*As she pours the rest of* MEG*'s ice into her cup*) Thanks. Uncle says we should live like God could be here any minute. What'll he think if he gets here, and we're canning beans for the winter?

MEG: What if he gets here, but winter got here first?

HANNAH: Why do you think he isn't coming?

MEG: I just think if he was, he'd've been here by now.

HANNAH: Uncle says people who think that way are basing it on emotions and inaccuracy. No rational person would believe something that she'll end up in hell if she's wrong. You've had a million chances to get back with God, and you won't even try.

MEG: I have tried, Hannah. Nothing happens. (*Beat*) What's praying like for you? Do you picture him?

HANNAH: I know he's looking down on me with love, but when I look back...I can't explain it.

MEG: Does he have a face?

HANNAH: Not exactly.

MEG: You can't *see* it, or he doesn't have one?

HANNAH: Why do you care?

MEG: Because *you* care. So how can you tell he loves you?

HANNAH: Because of how he's smiling. I can't see his face, but I know.

MEG: Show me.

(Beat. HANNAH *is clearly self-conscious)*

MEG: Don't be embarrassed. I just want to see what love looks like to you.

(Beat. HANNAH *closes her eyes. when she reopens them, her face is suffused with a relaxed warmth.* MEG *drinks it in.)*

MEG: Thank you. Maybe if he'd've smiled at me just once like that…

HANNAH: He didn't always smile. I was always making him angry, so Uncle and dad gave me Azazel.

SHEILA: *(From her office)* Azazel?

MEG: Hannah's goat.

JACK: Goats have many fine qualities. They're intelligent, sensitive and playful like you. but they can also be contrary…like you.

HANNAH: You want *me* to take care of him? He's the contrariest goat to ever kick down a door.

JACK: Uncle and I just thought whatever you do to tame him, a little might rub off on you.

MEG: Who named him Azazel?

HANNAH: Uncle. From Leviticus.

MEG: I know, "the scapegoat". When *he* got contrary, God threw him in a Lake of Fire.

HANNAH: Ask anyone…I'm the best milker at The Realm. They usually save the milk for the little kids, so their bones grow up straight, but I was pulling down so many gallons, Uncle said I deserve a cup every day with breakfast as a reward. Excuse me. *(Reaching towards her stomach, she turns and quickly starts to exit, then stops)* False alarm.

MEG: I'm just wondering, Hannah…that was the third time it's happened today, and since it's also the first morning visit / we've (had) …

HANNAH: They're just tummy rumbles. I get them as a caution against my vanity, and saying I'm the best milker was a brag.

MEG: Did you have any milk before you came?

HANNAH: There's nothing wrong with the milk. I always boil it right away.

MEG: When you were little, your favorite treat was a glass of milk with Bosco. After you started throwing up, we figured it was the Bosco, but the doctor said you're "lactose intolerant".

HANNAH: That was store milk, so it probably came from a cow.

MEG: You can get it with any mammal.

(Reacting to HANNAH's *blank expression:)*

MEG: A mammal… If you don't believe me, just stop drinking it a few days, and you'll know.

HANNAH: It's not the milk.

MEG: Or there's a pill you can take *before* you drink it.

HANNAH: I don't need a pill.

MEG: You pass right by a Walgreens. Just ask Mrs Pickett to get you this.

*(*MEG *writes on a slip of paper and gives it to* HANNAH, *then turns quickly to* SHEILA*)*

MEG: I knew she wouldn't ask, so I picked some up myself.

*(*MEG *picks up a large shopping bag, turns back to* HANNAH, *sets down the bag and takes out a small bottle of pills.)*

HANNAH: I asked Uncle, and *he* said God wouldn't reward me with something that makes me sick.

MEG: These pills won't either. The worst that can happen is *nothing'll* happen, so what do you have to lose?

(MEG *places bottle in front of* HANNAH, *who ignores it*)

MEG: Humor me.

(HANNAH *continues to ignore it*)

MEG: You'd rather keep getting sick than take a chance you'll find out Uncle is wrong?

HANNAH: He *isn't* wrong.

(*Frustrated,* MEG *reaches into the shopping bag and removes a 32 ounce, clear plastic glass and a quart of milk. She pours the entire quart, then discards the carton and gestures towards the glass.*)

MEG: If it's the milk, your whole insides will start screaming, but at least you'll know. (*She gets a second bowl and sets it in front of* HANNAH.) I wish you'd just believe me. I remember how much you hated throwing up.

HANNAH: You want me to drink it?

MEG: Yes. All of it.

HANNAH: This is a trick. If you really thought I'd get sick...

(*Searching* MEG's *face,* HANNAH *slowly raises the glass almost to her lips, then stops. After she gives* MEG *a final look, she is about to gulp it down, when* MEG *grabs her wrist.*)

MEG: (*Visibly shaken, she indicates the milk that spilled*) There are napkins in the bag. Would you? Before it dries.

(*As* HANNAH *gets them:*)

MEG: I'm sorry.

(MEG *turns, as* SHEILA *speaks:*)

SHEILA: Sorry for what? You didn't actually let her drink it.

MEG: You don't know how close…I kept wanting to scream, "I'm the parent! Why are you making this so hard?!" If I had waited one more second… What's wrong with me?

(HANNAH *has returned with napkins.* MEG *gets on her knees and begins to wipe it up.* HANNAH *watches, then surreptitiously slips the bottle into her pocket.*)

SHEILA: Did she try them?

MEG: She didn't say, and I didn't ask. But she hasn't needed the bathroom since.

(MEG *turns to* HANNAH, *as they move to the visit room*)

MEG: I was thinking about that blue Oldsmobile we drove to Hugo. What did dad call the blue?

HANNAH: Midnight blue.

MEG: "Midnight blue." You helped him fix it, when we got back.

HANNAH: The shop in town wanted to sell him a compressor, but it just needed new seals.

MEG: There must be a gene for speaking "car" you got from him. He was always saying things that made equally no sense to me.

(HANNAH *laughs. Beat*)

HANNAH: Did you love dad?

MEG: Back then, I did. Yes.

HANNAH: What about your friend Mr Schmidt with the sideburns who sometimes came over?

MEG: Jim Schmidt? He was *dad's* friend.

HANNAH: He brought you a whole bouquet of purple oxeye daisies when he came for dinner once.

MEG: I highly doubt they were for me, since his girlfriend always came too.

HANNAH: I don't think he liked her that way. The moment he'd start talking to you...

MEG: Did dad say this ?

HANNAH: I doubt he even noticed.

MEG: Noticed what?

HANNAH: How much happier you looked. You honestly weren't attracted to him?

MEG: I enjoyed Jim's conversation, but Dad was a hundred times better looking.

HANNAH: Then why wasn't he enough?

MEG: The thing you never understood...*Dad's* the one who cheated. I wasn't enough for *him*.

HANNAH: You thought *dad* was cheating? With who?

MEG: God. If dad could've kept it to...like a Sunday morning liaison... But he fell in love.

(MEG *turns to* JACK. *They are on the phone. Flashback. He looks ill and worn down from pain.*)

MEG: The letter says "I, Jack Thompson, am appointing Bountiful Blessings Church to be Hannah Thompson's legal guardian in the event I am unable to perform..." What *is* this?

JACK: What is what?

MEG: The letter from your lawyer that you signed.

JACK: I didn't get any letter.

(MEG *is clearly confused by* JACK's *response.*)

JACK: It's nice to hear your voice, Meg, but you know how mad Mr Lomax gets when we use the phone outside of breaks.

MEG: Jack...you don't work for Mr Lomax.

JACK: What do you mean?

MEG: You haven't for almost a year.

(MEG, *sensing* JACK's *distress:*)

MEG: It's okay, Jack. Are you on medication? That could be why. What did the doctor say?

JACK: I'm dying. I had something in my brain, but now it's all over me.

MEG: (*A surge of emotion, which she tries to cover*) Maybe he's wrong. You never believed in doctors before, why start now?

JACK: I've been praying I'll hold on long enough to see him with Hannah when he gets here.

MEG: Whatever happens, she's gonna need me now.

JACK: She'll still have the church.

MEG: Oh, Jack. I wish…I've always believed you're a good man inside, and if the church'd just left us alone, we'd've figured it out.

JACK: (*Starting to slip into a drug haze now*) The Realm is starting to bloom. There's a garden we're all supposed to meet / when it's…

MEG: Stay with me, Jack. You need to tell your lawyer you didn't realize what you were signing. If you give Uncle this kind of power, (then) …

JACK: *You* remember Hazel Jessup's garden. She's done a lot of the plantings, so / imagine…

MEG: Listen to me! I'm begging you. The church already took Hannah from me once…don't let it take her again.

JACK: (*Slipping further away*) I can't wait to see Hannah's face when he gets here. My only sorrow…I always thought when he finally came, you'd be waiting with us.

(Phone rings. MEG *turns, as if startled awake. Flashback)*

HANNAH: Mom?

MEG: Hannah? I can't believe… What is it, hon… Are you okay?

HANNAH: Dad isn't moving. I heard a crash, and he was just lying there.

MEG: Let me call Dr Bennett.

HANNAH: No. The Olsens are coming over with Dr Wood. If they knew I was calling you…

MEG: Did they say where Dr Wood is going to take him?

HANNAH: Mrs Olson suggested the hospital, but Dr Wood didn't want / (to do that)…

MEG: He can't. The hospital took his privileges…

HANNAH: I think they plan on keeping him here.

MEG: No. Under no circumstances… Call 9-1-1. The ambulance *has* to take him to a hospital.

HANNAH: I'm scared. Could you come here tonight?

MEG: Honey…I'm more than two hours…

HANNAH: If you leave right now…

MEG: Dad still has the restraining order, and he signed a letter, so if Uncle wants me arrested…

HANNAH: I can't listen to that now, I just need you to come.

MEG: Hannah, listen. Hopefully dad'll pull through, but if for whatever reason…things could be very different, and to risk all of that now…

HANNAH: So you're not coming?

MEG: I *am* coming…I promise. As soon as / I…

HANNAH: No, I need you *tonight*. You have to come /
tonight.

MEG: That's not gonna happen. I'm sorry, Hannah. I
can't. Not tonight.

(HANNAH *goes to visit room.* MEG *cautiously joins her.*)

HANNAH: He screamed for hours. I just sat there,
holding his hand.

MEG: Have you cried since he passed?

HANNAH: Why would I? He's in heaven now.

MEG: You can still feel sad.

(HANNAH *bursts into tears, then angrily chokes it off.*)

HANNAH: Why did you say that?!

MEG: Because you seem to think it's wrong.

HANNAH: It *is* wrong. I should be happy. He's not in
pain.

(HANNAH *and* MEG *both turn and step toward* JACK,
HANNAH *is remembering what follows, while* MEG *tries to
imagine it. As* HANNAH *takes* JACK's *hand,* MEG *touches
her shoulder.*)

HANNAH: Uncle tried to pray with him, but he kept
screaming. Mother Becca said it wasn't his fault.

MEG: Of course not. How could screaming in pain…?

HANNAH: It didn't make sense! He knew God would
be there any minute.

MEG: The pain must've been so intense, he forgot God
was even coming.

HANNAH: *(Her secret fear exploding out of her)* What if
someone came, but it wasn't God?

(HANNAH *sobs, then lets go of his hand to cover her ears. A
moment later,* JACK *screams. As* HANNAH *starts to collapse,*

MEG *grabs and hugs her tight. Darkness. When lights come up,* MEG *and* MRS PICKETT *are in the visit room.)*

MEG: So you're Mother Becca.

PICKETT: You don't remember me.

MEG: I just thought you're some driver named "Mrs Pickett". What do you need to tell me?

PICKETT: I also drove Hannah to visits when you came here from Brownwood, but I never came inside, because I was too... What's the word for when you don't say much?

(MEG just stares at PICKETT.)

PICKETT: This is hard.

MEG: Good, it should be. I don't know how you can sleep at night.

PICKETT: I used to take these little blue pills before bed, but then Uncle said I don't need them.

MEG: Do you have children? Of your own, I mean?

PICKETT: I have three womb children, but they're in Kansas with my husband.

MEG: Do you get to see them?

PICKETT: He said it was stirring up too many bad things from the past.

MEG: Fights about religion?

PICKETT: My people were meat and gravy Baptists, and P J handled snakes, but we mostly got along until my breakdown, when he started saying I'm a bad wife, because he did all the housework while I just sat on the couch hearing voices. Then one morning he shook me awake and said he was thinking of ditching me for someone named Beverly, but we had to run it by the pastor first. *(A couple of beats as she looks off silently.)*

MEG: So what did your pastor / say?

PICKETT: He said no one keeps getting visits from dark, unseen voices, unless she invited them, so my husband was free to cast me out. Two days later, Beverly had her things moved in and was already cleaning the house. *(Beat, looking off sadly)* Hannah said something in the car. *(She turns to HANNAH.)*

HANNAH: I wonder if a girl ever refused to live with her mother, but the judge still made her go. *(Slight beat)* Like maybe the girl said terrible things about her mother, but the judge went "Oh, she's just being a teenager" ...like that. *(Beat)* Could even be the girl who stood up and told the judge "You'll have to drag me", so when he made her go anyway, nobody blamed it on her.

(PICKETT steals a look at HANNAH, then looks ahead again.)

PICKETT: I guess if she talked to the judge in private *before* he made her go, no one could blame her, since no one would know what she said.

(HANNAH stares at PICKETT, surpised, then tries to hide her smile, as she considers this. PICKETT turns back to MEG.)

MEG: Why are you telling me this?

PICKETT: My voices said to. All my other pastors said "God hates crazy" and "Keep that demon talk away from my flock", but Uncle told me to heed their advice.

MEG: What if your voices disagree with something God told *him*?

PICKETT: I know God speaks through Uncle, but Uncle isn't his only voice.

MEG: You don't actually (mean) ...? Does anyone else there think Uncle isn't his only voice?

PICKETT: There's a kind of unspoken rule you don't ask, but I suspect there are a few.

MEG: If you don't believe every word Uncle says comes straight from God, why do you stay?

PICKETT: The people. So much of our life is waiting, it's a blessing to have nice people to wait with. Ever since you came back, my voices have been telling me to talk with you, so when God comes, I'll be clean for him. *(Beat)* That summer before you stopped visiting, there were storms like I'd never seen, but you never missed a visit…so later, when Hannah began saying hateful things, because she thought you abandoned her, I could've reminded her of those storms, but I didn't. I never *agreed*, but the Bible's pretty clear. "To him who knows to do good and does not do it…"

MEG: *(Finishing for her)* "To him it is sin." When my lawyer asked why she'd be better off living with me, I said, "How is that even a question?" Then one day I got here early, and I saw you praying with her. I knew I should leave until you finished, but I just stood there, watching you pray.

(Beat, as MEG *and* PICKETT *fully take each other in.)*

PICKETT: Do you remember those two women who brought King Solomon a baby? Each swore the baby was hers, so Solomon said he would cut it in half. He knew whichever woman was willing to give up the baby to save it was the real mother. Hannah told me you stopped her from drinking the milk.

MEG: I almost let her.

PICKETT: God knew the real mother would always stop her in time. *(She turns towards the waiting room.)* Hannah?

*(*HANNAH *enters. A couple of beats, then to* PICKETT:*)*

HANNAH: Just on the almost zero chance I go, what'll happen when God comes, and Uncle tells him where I've gone?

PICKETT: Don't worry, pumpkin. You won't have to give up God to live in Austin.

(Glancing at MEG, PICKETT *quietly exits.* HANNAH *explodes:)*

HANNAH: It'll *never* work! I won't know a single person, and everyone says Austin's like a noisy insane asylum.

MEG: People *are* louder there…and busier. It took some getting used to, but the flip side is they're…not smarter…but they *think* straighter, because they've been practicing logic their entire lives. You won't find another Bountiful Blessings exactly, but Austin has so many choices… Three blocks from us, there's a Pentecostal church, a Synagogue and some other group that had issues with *both* testaments, so they wrote their own, with a lot of poems on how God is what we feel when we walk on the beach.

HANNAH: Would I have to be in a special class for ignorant kids that don't know what a mammal is?

MEG: If everyone else knows, it can't be that hard to pick up. The principal said there's Bible study a block away. A lot of kids go straight from school. They just had a quiz on Joshua.

HANNAH: *(Delighted with herself)* Joshua's so easy, I got a hundred on that!

*(*MEG *turns to* SHEILA.*)*

MEG: I think she's close. If I could have two more visits…

SHEILA: I know, but tomorrow's all you've got. Here's a list of questions the judge'll probably ask her, so leave time to go over them. No matter how sure she feels, it's one thing to tell *you* and another to tell the judge.

MEG: I think once she finally meets him, and they're alone, she'll be fine.

SHEILA: They won't be alone. This all happens in open court.

(SHEILA *realizes this is news to* MEG.)

MEG: Can people from the church come?

SHEILA: That's what open court means. Anyone can come. *(Slight beat)* All this judge knows is she's been saying she hates you for two years, and all of a sudden... What if a month from now she changes her mind again...? The only way she'll convince him she's serious is to look at the people she's leaving and explain it to *them*.

MEG: I'll bet the church is pressuring him to make this as hard as possible.

SHEILA: The church had nothing to do with it. It was me.

(MEG *stares at* SHEILA, *stunned.*)

SHEILA: If Hannah chooses you, but nobody's hears her, he'll just keep doing it to other kids.

MEG: That's not *her* problem.

SHEILA: Sorry?

(*A sudden chasm has opened between* MEG *and* SHEILA.)

MEG: I can't ask her to stand up in front of everyone she knows...

SHEILA: Of course you can. Take some credit, she trusts you now.

MEG: That church has been her entire life.

SHEILA: I can't believe this. Now that she finally *wants* to go... You still want *her*, don't you?

MEG: Of course, but if it makes her life *worse*...
Religion's the only way she has of seeing the world,
and I can't even say grace with her.

SHEILA: So she'll be better off with them?

MEG: I didn't say she'll be better / (off with) ...

SHEILA: Good, so can we look at those questions?

MEG: I'll just tell her how much I want us to be
together, and I hope she wants that too, but if she can't
handle saying it in front of everyone, I'll understand.

SHEILA: No, you won't. You'll tell her whatever the
church does to punish her, you know she's strong
enough to handle it.

MEG: I don't know that. She's sixteen. How strong is
anyone at that age?

SHEILA: So after everything these people put you
through, you're ready to risk losing your daughter just
to spare her the awkwardness of upsetting them?

MEG: The *"awkwardness"*?

(*Beat,* MEG *and* SHEILA *stare at each other, both furious.*)

MEG: Now I know why you don't have any pictures in
here of your kids? You don't have any, do you?

SHEILA: (*Beat*) The first time I took on a church, there
was a twelve year-old boy who needed a simple
operation to keep his kidneys from shutting down. His
church believed only absolute faith in God's power
could save him, so rather than take him to a doctor, his
parents asked a faith healer to pray over him instead.
When the boy got worse, the *father* finally broke down
and started taking him to a doctor, until the mother
found out and stopped him, so the father asked me to
get a court order for the operation. The judge asked the
doctor if he could say with absolute certainty that the
operation would save the boy's life. When of course

he couldn't, the judge ruled that his medical opinion,
like the faith healer's belief in prayer, was ultimately
an act of faith, so both should be given equal weight,
and the mother...who had always stayed home with
the boy...should decide. When the boy died a month
later, the church blamed the father and refused to let
him attend the funeral. The mother...*and* their two
other children...haven't spoken to him since. I still call
to see how he's doing, and to this day, he believes the
church was right. *(Beat)* I have two boys, but you won't
see pictures, because most parents who come here
have lost their children or are terrified they will... They
don't need to see happy pictures of mine. Hannah's
your daughter, so naturally you think her feelings
are important. Trust me, they're not. No more than
my two or any others, but Hannah has a chance to *do*
something important, which is help me stop any *more*
kids from being stolen in the name of some God who
can't possibly be real, because no *real* God would stand
for it.

(MEG turns to visit room, where HANNAH is clearly upset.)

HANNAH: You realize if I do what you're asking,
everyone'll hate me?

MEG: It's the only way the judge will let you go.

HANNAH: Then give me a reason to go.

MEG: We went over that last time.

HANNAH: "People in Austin are logical, and there's
Bible study after school." Are those what you're calling
"reasons"?

MEG: They're not the only... The school won an
award... You'll have your own room... What can I *say*,
Hannah? I have a dozen like that, but they're all just
... "advantages" ...not *reasons*. I never knew I *needed*
reasons. I just thought, "I'm your mother, you should

be with me", it was that simple. And as stupid as that sounds, I still believe it.

(Slight beat)

I know there are plenty of people at the Realm who genuinely care about you. They can pray with you, because they believe, and I can't give you that. But they won't *get* you like me. They can't possibly love you as much, because they'll never understand the "unbelieving" parts of you. I'm the only one who will always love all of you.

HANNAH: *(Beat)* I was sneaking a peak at my hands today to see which thumb was on top, and I realized the two of us also…like when I do this. *(She taps her index finger three times against her cheek)* You do it right after you say something you wish you hadn't. Try it.

(As HANNAH *does,* MEG *is surprised to discover* HANNAH *is right.)*

HANNAH: I know, it's weird. Do you ever have questions, when you ask them, people look at you like this? *(She gives an exaggerated blank stare.)* Like when God comes, will everyone have to die before he can take us, so we'll all start falling off roofs or having heart attacks at the same time? Will everyone be the same age in heaven, or can we choose? Uncle once said God'll make us shiny and new, so I thought maybe we'll all look like babies, but that can't be right.

MEG: I don't have *those* questions, but I get the same look with mine.

HANNAH: Is that a reason to go with you? It seems more like a reason not to. Mother Tammy says every important question has an answer in the Bible, and those should satisfy me.

MEG: Do they?

HANNAH: See? This is exactly why you'd be a terrible influence. If I live with you, you'll be constantly throwing in little comments like that to make believing sound dumb.

MEG: I don't think believing is dumb. If I'd been given a choice to either believe everything the church said or just what made sense to me, I'd've picked "everything" hands down. I tried to believe that way for years, and when I realized I couldn't, I pretended. As long as I did it so they couldn't tell, nobody gave me that look.

HANNAH: How come you stopped pretending?

MEG: Different reasons. Jim Schmidt for one, and no, I wasn't attracted, so don't start. I liked how he could laugh at things we weren't supposed to. I once asked him why he bothered going to church, since he spent half the time cracking jokes under his breath about religion, and he said he got more satisfaction poking fun at something he loved than things he didn't care. One night he told a joke that was so profane I thought the sky would split open but so funny food came out my nose. We all thought we'd die laughing, and dad laughed harder than anyone. I think that's why he never invited Jim back. *(Slight beat)* If you need *one* reason to leave, you won't lose all those years, pretending like me.

(As MEG *moves to the side,* HANNAH *walks downstage, slowly removing her bonnet, then her frock, revealing a simple, floral print dress.* SHEILA *enters, holding out a bible, as* HANNAH *turns and puts her hand on it.)*

HANNAH: I do.

SHEILA: If you could turn to look at all the decent, God fearing people who are here today, praying you'll decide… If you could that *now*? And direct your answers to them.

(HANNAH *hesitates, then turns to face downstage.*)

SHEILA: If the court allows you to move, are you prepared to never see these people again?

HANNAH: During my earthly years, yes.

SHEILA: You understand that in being desanctified, you'll be erased from their hearts.

HANNAH: But they'll...*you'll* still be in mine, along with everything you taught me. So when I'm out in the fallen world, I'll have that with me. And when we're in heaven, those years will be like a few cross words spoken in a moment of anger and just as quickly forgotten.

SHEILA: Do you believe when God comes, he'll take only the faithful and leave the rest behind?

HANNAH: That's what I was taught, and I have no evidence to doubt it.

SHEILA: So you understand by choosing to live with your mother, the most you can hope for is a few short years before you lose her again, only this time for eternity.

HANNAH: That was my fear, *before* I started to pray on it. Now I know she'll be in heaven too.

SHEILA: You honestly believe God would overlook...? Sorry, your Honor, but I think it *is* relevant to whether she's thought her decision through. (*Back to* HANNAH) How will your mother get to heaven if, as she's told you, she can't even pray?

HANNAH: My mom used to believe, and God commands us to turn those who have lost their way towards him again. (*Turning to face* MEG) I will *personally* see to it that my mother gets there.

(SHEILA *exits.* HANNAH *goes to* MEG.)

HANNAH: You promise you'll take me to any church I pick and wait till I'm ready to leave?

MEG: I promise.

HANNAH: And come inside with me whenever I ask?

MEG: If I have to.

HANNAH: You swore you'll try God again. The whole courtroom heard you.

MEG: What else could I say? I mean, yes.

HANNAH: The judge wrote it down, so you'll be breaking the law if you don't.

MEG: I actually tried that church with the nature poems once, but thanking the beach didn't do any more for me than thanking an old man in the sky.

HANNAH: Promise.

MEG: *(Beat)* Okay. Just try to find something with a choir.

(A song like Generation Why *by Weyes Blood could play. For a moment,* JACK *appears to* HANNAH *as the healthy vigorous man he once was, then quickly disappears.* HANNAH *turns back to* MEG, *and they hug.)*

END OF PLAY

www.ingramcontent.com/pod-product-compliance
Lightning Source LLC
Chambersburg PA
CBHW052204090426
42741CB00010B/2399